The Ketogenic Cookbook

55 of The Easiest and Most Delicious Ketogenic Recipes on the Planet

Sara Elliott Price

Published in The USA by:

Success Life Publishing

125 Thomas Burke Dr.

Hillsborough, NC 27278

Copyright © 2015 by Sara Elliott Price

ISBN-10: 1511872128

Disclaimer

Every effort has been made to accurately represent this book and its potential. Results vary with every individual, and your results may or may not be different from those depicted. No promises, guarantees or warranties, whether stated or implied, have been made that you will produce any specific result from this book. Your efforts are individual and unique, and may vary from those shown. Your success depends on your efforts, background and motivation.

The material in this publication is provided for educational and informational purposes only and is not intended as medical advice. The information contained in this book should not be used to diagnose or treat any illness, metabolic disorder, disease or health problem. Always consult your physician or health care provider before beginning any nutrition or exercise program. Use of the programs, advice, and information contained in this book is at the sole choice and risk of the reader.

Table of Contents

Introduction

Why the ketogenic diet?

High Fat for Life

Farmers feed their livestock grain in order to fatten the animals up. Experimentally, a group of farmers tried feeding their pigs coconut oil (because science at the time held that fat causes weight gain) and the effort backfired. The pigs lost weight and were observed to be more active than ever before.

A young boy suffering from severe epileptic seizures used a high-fat diet to get his seizures under control (His family discovered the ketogenic diet and applied it to get great results). The seizures eventually went away entirely and he was healed. Others report getting acne and other skin problems completely under wraps using this diet. Parkinson's, cancer, multiple sclerosis and other conditions are among those a high fat, low carbohydrate diet can treat.

Ketones for the Win

Ketones are a metabolic unit created when the level of glucose in the body has fallen below a certain point. The ketones trigger the body to flood the liver with fatty acids. The fat reserves in the body are used as fuel to power bodily functions.

Thus, weight is lost. This process also deprives cancer cells and other abnormal cells in the body of food (as glucose is required for fermentation to feed these oxidants and invaders). This fuels health, and not sickness.

The Ketogenic Diet

The ketogenic diet follows the creed that natural fats are healthy fuel for the body. The diet triggers the body to switch from running on sugar, to running on fat. Following the recipes included in this e-book will help you to get to the point where your body burns off its fat reserves. In order to do that, you need to hold to the ratio of 4:1 fats to carbohydrates and proteins. Don't worry, you don't need to constantly do math to succeed at the diet: you do need to follow recipes and guidelines of foods you shouldn't eat and moderate your portions of protein, and extremely limit your portions of carbohydrates. (If you eat too many carbs, your body will fall out of ketosis and you will have to start over from square one).

Getting started can be a daunting task. One has to first consider what can and cannot be eaten, what quantity it can be eaten in and when. This cook book will help relieve a lot of that stress and give you easy, delicious recipes you can make right at home. This book is an easy reference for those wondering where to start, and more importantly: what to eat? You can come up with your own meal plan using the recipes in this book. We've tried to keep things as simple as possible, while providing delicious and nutritious meals that are 100% ketogenic.

In order to reap the rewards of as many health benefits as possible, we recommend using organic ingredients wherever possible. If you are not able to find them, then this will not affect ketosis or the effects of the diet. Prefer organic, non-GMO ingredients purchased locally whenever you can.

Your body will thank you, and you will never be as pleased with the reflection in the mirror or how you feel. Prevent cancer, get great skin and achieve your ideal weight!

Before we get to the recipes, let's take a look at some of the foods that can and cannot be eaten on this diet.

Foods to absolutely cut out of your diet:

Refined sugar - Cake, cookies, candies are all not allowed.

High-sugar fruit - Bananas are not part of the ketogenic diet. Other tropical fruits such as mangos, pineapples and papaya are also high-sugar and as such are not allowed.

Bread and grains - Noodles, rolls, and other such high-carb grain products are not part of the diet.

Foods that are encouraged:

Eat plenty of fats like butter, coconut oil, lard, olive oil.

Water. Drink plenty of water!

Satisfying Breakfast Recipes

This first recipe is totally easy and satisfying. These treats are perfect to prepare and enjoy at breakfast.

Ketogenic Bacon and Eggs
(Good for two)

Ingredients:

- 6 eggs
- 8 bacon slices
- 2/3 of a cup full fat (heavy) cream
- Salt, pepper, oregano to taste
- Chopped garlic (optional)
- Butter for frying
- 1 Sliced avocado and 1 tomato with a drizzle of olive oil

Procedure:

1. In a bowl, combine the eggs and the cream. Whisk together. Add the salt, pepper, chopped garlic to the egg and cream mixture.
2. In a frying pan, fry bacon over medium heat. Transfer to a plate.
3. Add the eggs to the bacon grease, along with the butter.
4. Being careful not to overcook the eggs, stir with a spatula or wooden spoon.

5. When the eggs have reached the desired consistency, serve them along with the bacon and the sliced tomato and avocado and olive oil (each person receives half: this is important in order to keep the ketogenic state. Don't overeat!)

Enjoy!

This next recipe combines the fall-favorite that is all things pumpkin (which is healthy for every time of year) with high fat cream cheese.

Ketogenic Pumpkin Pancakes

Ingredients:

- 2 ounces of cream cheese
- 1 cup of organic pumpkin (can be bought canned, but you can make your own if you like)
- 2 eggs
- A few drops of stevia
- Pumpkin pie spices (cinnamon, nutmeg, ginger)
- Butter for frying

Procedure:

1. Combine the cream cheese, pumpkin and eggs in a bowl. Use a hand mixture to combine to a smooth mixture. Add the spices and the stevia and distribute throughout.
2. Add the butter to the pan and melt.
3. Pour pancake sized batter to the pan. When the edges are firm enough, flip with a spatula to cook evenly on both sides.
4. Serve with butter and bacon.
5. Enjoy!

Since grains aren't allowed on the ketogenic diet, we have to be creative to find delicious, fulfilling equivalents to the morning favorite that is porridge. This rich porridge combines almond meal with heavy cream for a delectable morning experience.

Ketogenic Porridge

Ingredients:

- 2 cups of almond meal
- 2 cups of heavy cream (or the amount preferred to achieve the desired consistency of the porridge)
- 1 egg
- Coconut oil
- A few drops of stevia
- Cinnamon or vanilla powder (optional)
- A couple raspberries or blueberries to garnish

Procedure:

1. Combine the almond meal, heavy cream and egg in a sauce pan over low heat. Stirring occasionally, warm the ingredients.
2. Add the coconut oil, drops of stevia and spices. Cook until you have achieved a creamy, thick porridge

consistency. (You may add water or more cream to make it a thinner consistency if you wish).

3. Serve in a bowl, with a few raspberries or another type of low-sugar berry. You can also top with butter for an extra rich taste. (Recommended)

This next recipe is for a wonderful treat that is also totally keto and amazing! Spicy muffins to eat for breakfast are so good you could also eat them for dessert.

Ketogenic Almond Morning Muffins

Ingredients:

- 6 eggs
- 2/3 of a cup almond flour
- ¼ cup almond or macadamia butter
- ¼ cup full fat cream
- 2 tablespoons of coconut oil
- 1 tablespoon of butter
- A pinch of salt, cinnamon, nutmeg and vanilla
- 12 drops of stevia
- 1-2 cups of whipping cream, if so desired (to top with)

Procedure:

1. Preheat your oven to 350 degrees Fahrenheit.

2. Mix the almond flour and spices.

3. Place the almond butter, coconut oil and butter together in dish. Fill a pan with hot water and put the dish into the pan to melt the coconut oil and butter and soften the almond butter.

4. Add the coconut oil, butter and almond butter to the flour combination. Then add eggs, stevia and cream and mix thoroughly.

5. Grease a muffin pan or place muffin cups in the pan. Pour the mixture into the cups and place in the oven.

6. Bake for 25 minutes.

7. Serve with whipped cream or melted butter as a topping. Low-sugar berries also make a great topping.

This next recipe is a bread recipe. You can slice up the loaf and use the bread for sandwiches, eat it with butter and bacon for breakfast, or simply as is for a quick snack on the go.

Ketogenic Loaf of Bread

Ingredients:

- 4 eggs
- 100 grams of almond flour
- 2 teaspoons of baking powder
- A half a stick of butter

Procedure:

1. Preheat the oven to 350 degrees Fahrenheit.
2. Combine the ingredients in a large bowl. Stir or mix with a hand mixer until all the ingredients are smooth.
3. In a greased bread pan, pour the batter.
4. Place in the oven and bake for 20-25 minutes or until golden brown.

This recipe is a dream for lovers of Mexican food and bacon! It is perfect for weekends, or prepared the night before for eating on the go. It's also delicious for dinner! (Or whenever you feel like eating it!)

Ketogenic Breakfast Burrito

Ingredients:

- 1 pound of ground beef
- 1 onion
- 2 cloves of garlic
- Butter for frying
- 1 tablespoon of cayenne pepper
- 1 cup of tomato paste or sugar-free tomato sauce
- 1 pinch of pepper
- Mexican style shredded cheese
- 1 cup of sour cream
- Sliced avocado

Procedure:

1. Brown the ground beef in the butter. Add the onions and the garlic and the cayenne as well as the pepper. Simmer along with the tomato paste.
2. Pre-heat the oven to 350 degrees.
3. In an oven safe dish, lay out four strips of bacon overlapping (Google bacon weave if unsure how to perform this.
4. Put a few spoonfuls of ground beef on top of this, along with a sprinkling of Mexican cheese.

5. Wrap the beef up in the bacon. Repeat this until all of the bacon is used.
6. Bake in the oven until the bacon is crispy. Serve with avocado and sour cream

This next breakfast recipe requires baking the bread using the recipe that appears elsewhere in this book.

Ketogenic French Toast

Bread prepared from the ketogenic bread recipe that appears in this book

Ingredients:

- 12 slices of bacon
- 1 cup of sour cream
- 2 eggs
- 1 cup of heavy cream
- 1 teaspoon of cinnamon and 1 teaspoon of nutmeg
- Butter for frying

Procedure:

1. Melt the butter in a frying pan.
2. Mix the cream and eggs and spices.
3. Slice the bread.
4. Lay a slice of bread in the egg mixture. Flip so the other side is coated. Fry in the frying pan with butter. Repeat the process.
5. Serve with whipped cream and a few berries.

Scrumptious Lunch Recipes

This first recipe is for an easy but delightful salad you will love to take with you to work to eat for lunch.

Ketogenic BLT Salad

Ingredients:

- 6 slices of bacon
- 1 large tomato
- ½ a cucumber
- 1 head of lettuce (iceberg, romaine, green leaf, red leaf)
- Full fat yoghurt (for dressing)
- Garlic powder
- Onion powder
- Salt and pepper
- Olive oil

Procedure:

1. Fry the bacon over the stovetop. Leave to cool on a plate or a cutting board with a towel underneath (to keep the cutting board clean). Cut into bite size pieces.
2. Slice the tomato, cucumber. Cut the lettuce into bite size pieces

3. Mix the yoghurt with the garlic powder and onion powder. This is your dressing.

4. Put the tomato, cucumber and lettuce into a bowl along with the chopped bacon. Top with the yoghurt dressing. Stir to combine well. Drizzle a bit of olive oil on top. Sprinkle with salt and pepper. Bon appétit!

Here's a simple recipe that is inspired by a yummy Spanish favorite, altered for a new taste.

Cold-Stuffed Ketogenic Peppers

Ingredients:

- 2 red bell peppers drizzled with olive oil
- 2 cups of cream cheese
- 1 cup of cubed ham

Procedure:

1. Cut the peppers lengthwise in half. Remove the tops.
2. Mix the cream cheese with the ham.
3. Fill the peppers with the cream cheese and ham mixture. Serve with a little green salad, or eat on the go.

Here's a lunch recipe that's fast and delicious! Veggies and bacon combine with cheese for a ketogenic experience that's simply divine!

Cream Cheese and Bacon Ketogenic Cucumber Sandwich

Ingredients:

- 1 cucumber
- 1 cup of cream cheese
- 4 slices of bacon
- Butter for frying

Procedure:

1. Melt the butter in a pan over the stovetop. Add the bacon and fry until crispy.
2. Cut the cucumber lengthwise in half. Then cut in the middle.
3. When the bacon is ready and has been allowed to cool for a few minutes, cut it into little bits.
4. In a bowl, combine the bacon bits with the cream cheese.
5. Spread the bacon and cream cheese mixture over each piece of cucumber. Enjoy with a few slices of avocado.

Here we have a recipe for an easy and simple lunch. Anyone can make it, even those who feel eluded by scrambled eggs.

Ketogenic Turkey and Cheese Rolls

Ingredients:

- Sliced turkey(from your own roast, or from cold cuts)
- A nice fatty cheese such as cheddar cut in thin slices
- Half an avocado
- Whole stalks of chives

Procedure:

1. Cut up the turkey into fairly small pieces. If using cold cuts, roll them up.
2. Top the turkey with a piece of avocado.
3. Wrap the turkey and avocado combination with the cheese.
4. Tie a stalk of chive around the turkey and cheese roll ups.
5. Enjoy!

Here's a ketogenic "pasta" dish that's full of yummy fat, healthy vegetables and is very satisfying to eat, and simple to make. You can take it with you to work to eat, or eat this for dinner or a special lunch at home on the weekend. Double up the recipe as needed for several people. This recipe is best suited to two people.

Ketogenic Zucchini Noodle Alfredo

Ingredients:

- 2 zucchinis
- 2 tablespoons of butter
- 2 cups of heavy cream
- 4 tablespoons of parmesan cheese
- A handful of cherry tomatoes, sliced in half
- Shredded cheese of your choice (such as mozzarella)
- Some olive oil
- Salt and pepper
- Garlic powder

Procedure:

1. Using a zucchini noodle tool (spiralizer) or vegetable peeler, create thin strands out of the zucchini.

2. Over the stove, melt the butter. Fry the zucchini noodles quickly in the butter, then remove from heat.

3. In a bowl, combine the heavy cream, the parmesan and the salt and pepper, and the cherry tomatoes. Mix the cream and the cheese are evenly distributed and coating all of the "noodles".

4. In a baking dish, place the noodle mixture.

5. Top with shredded cheese.

6. Add a bit of olive oil on the top of the whole mixture.

7. Melt the cheese and warm the dish in the oven at 350 degrees Fahrenheit until the cheese is melted.

This next recipe is a delicious ketogenic take on an Italian favorite!

Ketogenic Tomato Sauce and Noodles

Ingredients:

- 2 zucchini cut into noodles
- 1 can of sugar-free tomato sauce
- 2 tablespoons of parmesan cheese
- Olive oil for frying
- 2 cloves of garlic

Procedure:

1. In a frying pan, add the garlic with olive oil. Sautee. Add the zucchini noodles and sautee them as well.
2. Add the tomato sauce and warm.
3. Remove from heat and sprinkle with parmesan cheese.

Here comes a super simple and great lunch recipe!

Ketogenic Tuna Salad

Ingredients:

- 1 can of organic white tuna
- A stalk of celery
- 3 tablespoons of Mayonaise (be careful that it is without ANY type of sugar, fructose, agave, etc)
- A tablespoon of heavy cream
- A pinch of pepper
- A squeeze of lemon juice
- A few leaves of lettuce

Procedure:

1. Open the can of tuna and remove the contents. Add the mayonnaise and the cream and stir to combine.
2. Chop up the celery into bite size pieces. Add to the tuna mixture. Stir to distribute evenly.
3. Squeeze the lemon juice into the tuna salad.
4. Serve over the lettuce leaves and enjoy.

Another easy salad, the flavor of Spanish tapas inclusive!

Ketogenic Spanish salad

Ingredients:

- Sliced chorizo Spanish sausage
- ½ cup of Spanish olives
- Red bell pepper or sweet red pepper cut into bits
- Your choice of lettuce (or baby spinach)
- Olive oil to top
- Some seasonings (salt, pepper, garlic powder, onion powder)

Procedure:

1. Slice the chorizo if you haven't purchased it that way. Cut up the olives into small bite-sized pieces.
2. Chop the peppers.
3. Chop the lettuce into bite size pieces.
4. Combine all of the above ingredients in a salad bowl.
5. Top with olive oil and seasonings, mix together or toss to distribute the oil and seasonings evenly.

Mouth-Watering Dinner Recipes

To kick off our collection of yummy dinner recipes, we have a dish which can be added to a lot of other dishes (such as ketogenic sandwiches, salads, zucchini noodles, etc). It is as versatile as it is rich and full of taste!

<u>Ketogenic Meatballs</u>

Ingredients:

- 1 pound of ground beef (or ground pork, or ground lamb)
- ½ cup of parmesan
- 1 tablespoon of garlic
- ½ cup of mozzarella cheese
- A pinch of salt and pepper and oregano if so desired

Procedure:

1. In a large bowl, combine all of the ingredients.
2. Roll the ingredients up into meatballs.
3. In a frying pan, melt butter.
4. Fry the meatballs in the butter.
5. To ensure they are cooked through, transfer to an oven safe pan and bake at 400 degrees Fahrenheit for 20 minutes.

Tip 1: A smaller size meatball is easier to cook through and be certain that the inside also reaches the right temperature.

Tip 2: Serve with zucchini noodles and sugar-free (an absolute must!) tomato sauce, or heavy cream sauce.

Ordinary rice is not allowed on the ketogenic diet. No problem! We have a delicious substitute for you, included in this next recipe.

Lemon Pepper Ketogenic Chicken with "Rice"

Ingredients:

- 2 breasts of chicken
- 1 lemon
- 1 tablespoon of freshly ground pepper
- 1 head of cauliflower
- Butter for frying
- Garlic powder
- Onion powder
- 1 cup of heavy cream

Procedure:

1. In a frying pan, melt the butter. Add the chicken filets and cook over medium heat.
2. Add the garlic and onion powder.
3. Add the pepper. Cut the lemon, and squeeze the lemon juice over the chicken. (Use three to four slices for this purpose and save the rest to garnish)

4. Cut the cauliflower into florets. Place in a food processor and spin until the cauliflower is in rice-sized pieces. Mix with the heavy cream. (No need to warm it up, but you may do so quickly in a saucepan if you so wish. Be careful to not overcook, a minute or two at low heat is enough).

5. When the chicken is ready, serve atop the cauliflower "rice". Sprinkle with a bit of Himalaya salt and additional pepper to taste.

6. Serve with a baby spinach salad (with a drizzle of olive oil and salt and pepper) on the side.

Enjoy!

This next recipe is a new take on a comfort-food favorite!

Cheesy Ketogenic Meatloaf

Ingredients:

- 1 pound of ground beef
- 1 egg
- 2 scallions (green onions)
- 1 yellow onion
- 2 cloves of garlic
- 2 cups of shredded mozzarella cheese, or fresh mozzarella sliced
- 1 cup of mascarpone cheese
- 2 cups of sugar free tomato sauce (or tomato paste or tomato passata (sugar free and without added ingredients)
- A pinch of seasonings (oregano, garlic powder, onion powder, cayenne pepper, paprika pepper, salt, pepper may all be used-don't use more than a pinch of each)

Procedure:

1. Preheat your oven to 400 degrees Fahrenheit.
2. Mix the ground beef and the egg in a large bowl.
3. Chop the garlic, onion and scallions and then add them to the egg and beef mixture. Stir well to combine.
4. Add the seasonings and stir again.

5. Mix the two types of cheese.

6. Roll out the beef on a sheet of plastic wrap on top of a cutting board so that it forms a flat sheet. Top the sheet and roll up (like a sandwich wrap so that the cheese is in the middle of the meatloaf).

7. In a greased tin or baking pan, place the meatloaf roll. Top with the tomato sauce and an extra sprinkling of mozzarella.

8. The inside will be a creamy, rich consistency and the outside traditional meatloaf. Delicious!

Ketogenic Stuffed peppers

Ingredients:

- 3 green peppers
- 4 sausages
- Butter for frying
- 2 eggs
- 2 ounces of parmesan cheese
- 2 ounces of cream cheese
- 1 yellow onion
- 2 cloves of garlic
- Seasonings to taste (a pinch of pepper and salt, thyme, etc)
- Olive oil for baking the peppers

Procedure:

1. Pre-heat the oven to 350 degrees Fahrenheit.
2. Cut the top (with the stem) off of the peppers. Cut them in half.
3. Cut the sausages up, removing the outer casing.
4. Fry the sausages in a pan with some melted butter. Add the eggs, and the two types of cheese.
5. Chop the onion and garlic, and add them to the mixture over the stovetop along with your choice of seasoning.
6. Stir to combine evenly.

7. Place the peppers in an oven-safe pan. Drizzle with olive oil, then top with the sausage-mixture filling.
8. Bake in the oven until the peppers are soft.

Bacon Tacos

Ingredients:

- 12 strips of bacon
- 1 pound of ground beef
- Seasonings of onion powder, garlic powder, cayenne pepper, paprika pepper
- A few leaves of iceberg lettuce
- One large tomato
- 1 cup of cheddar cheese
- ½ cup of sour cream

Procedure:

1. To make the bacon taco shells, on a paper towel, weave bacon strips together so they overlap on the paper towel. In the middle put some object to keep the mouth of the taco open (that is also microwave safe). Place everything in a microwave safe dish and microwave on high for about 5 minutes.
2. Brown the ground beef and add the seasoning.
3. Chop the lettuce and tomato into bite size bits.
4. When the bacon taco shells are ready and the meat is browned, allow to cool a bit and then add the meat to the shells. Top with the lettuce, tomato and cheese and sour cream.

Bone broth is very healthy for the digestion, and can also be made the following way, as a ketogenic meal that is good for the skin, hair, nails.

Bone Broth Soup(Ketogenic and Healthy Meal)

Ingredients:

- Beef bones, turkey bones or chicken bones (preferably with the meat still on)
- 3 celery stalks
- 1 large onion, chopped
- Scallions
- 1 carrot
- 1 knoll of fennel
- Seasoning: salt, pepper, garlic powder, onion powder
- ½ stick of butter

Procedure:

1. In a frying pan, melt a bit of the butter. Fry the chopped onion.
2. In a large pot, fill with water. Add the bones and the meat. Cook over low heat for 6 hours.
3. After 6 hours, add the vegetables: chopped carrot, fennel, celery, scallions and seasoning.
4. Simmer over low heat for another hour.

5. Serve and enjoy, store leftovers.

Ketogenic Taco Supreme Dinner Salad

Ingredients:

- 1 pound of ground beef (or pork, or Lamb)
- Seasonings of salt, pepper, onion powder, garlic powder, cayenne.
- 1 cup of tomato paste
- 2 tomatoes
- 1 head of lettuce
- 2 cups of sour cream
- 2 cups of cheddar cheese
- A bit of olive oil

Procedure:

1. Brown the ground beef over the stovetop in a frying pan. Add the seasonings and the tomato paste.
2. Chop the tomatoes and the lettuce. Add them to a large salad bowl.
3. When the meat is browned, allow to cool.
4. Top the lettuce and tomato salad with the meat, sour cream and the cheese.

Here's a ketogenic pizza recipe that also gets in helpings of healthy veggies, besides being amazingly good!

KetogenicCauliflower Pizza

Ingredients:

- 1 large head of cauliflower, chopped
- 2 tablespoons of butter
- 1 large onion, chopped
- ¼ cup of water
- 3 eggs
- 2 cups of shredded mozzarella cheese
- ½ cup of parmesan
- Sugar-free, low carb tomato or pizza sauce
- 2 cups of shredded Italian cheese

Procedure:

1. Preheat the oven to 400 degrees Fahrenheit. Cover a baking pan or cookie sheet with butter, lard or olive oil to grease it.
2. Lightly sauté the onions with the cauliflower. Add the ¼ cup of water and allow the cauliflower to cook. Then remove from heat, and allow to cool.

3. Once the cauliflower and onion mixture has cooled, pour into a food processer along with the eggs and the 2 cups of mozzarella cheese and the ½ cup of parmesan. Process until a smooth mixture has been formed.
4. Spread the cauliflower and cheese mixture onto the baking pan or cookie sheet.
5. Put the pan into the oven and bake for 25 minutes.
6. Pull the pan out and cover with the tomato sauce and the 2 cups of Italian blend cheese. (Another topping that is ketogenic approved is pepperoni and sausage. Feel free to add that to your pizza).
7. Bake until the cheese is melted.
8. Serve with a little green salad (lettuce and olive oil) as a delicious and hearty dinner.

This next dinner recipe is for a hearty steak, with a yummy bacon cream sauce and veggies on the side. Easy for beginners to prepare and enjoy.

Ketogenic Steak Dinner with Bacon Cream Sauce

Ingredients:

- Butter for frying
- 8 strips of bacon
- 2 steaks (beef or pork)
- 2 cups heavy cream
- 1 cup of sliced crimini mushrooms
- Broccoli and asparagus as a side

Procedure:

1. Fry the bacon in the butter. (The butter isn't necessary, but you may eat as much fat as you want on this diet, so why not?)
2. Add the mushrooms to the bacon frying and sauté them as well.
3. Add the cream to the mushroom and bacon mix.
4. In another pan, melt butter.

5. Add the steaks and fry until the steaks are cooked to the desired degree (medium, medium well, well done, etc)

6. In a saucepan, lightly steam broccoli and asparagus.

7. Serve the steaks with the bacon-mushroom-cream sauce and the broccoli and asparagus on the side.

Here's a great one for chicken lovers. Easy to prepare gourmet!

Ketogenic Chicken in White Wine Cream Sauce

Ingredients:

- A stick of butter
- 2 white onions
- 3 cloves of garlic
- ½ cup of homemade chicken broth (this is important as you need to ensure it is sugar free. Otherwise omit this ingredient).
- ½ cup of white wine
- 9 ounces of cream cheese
- ¼ cup heavy cream
- 1 teaspoon of your choice of seasoning
- A pinch of salt
- 4 chicken breasts

Procedure:

1. Fry the onions and garlic in 2 tablespoons of the butter. Remove from heat and place in another dish.
2. In the same pan, add the cream cheese, the cream, wine, 3 more tablespoons of butter and seasoning. Stir until melted and well combined.

3. Preheat the oven to 375 degrees Fahrenheit. Place the chicken in an oven safe dish along with 2 tablespoons of butter and the chicken broth. (If omitting the chicken broth, add more butter instead).

4. Cover the chicken filets with the onion and garlic mixture.

5. Then pour the cream sauce evenly over the filets.

6. Bake in the oven for 40-60 minutes.

7. Enjoy with a small green salad.

This next dish is simple, full of flavor, and the taste of India.
Best of all, it is totally ketogenic!

Ketogenic Indian Curry

Ingredients:

- 2 pounds of chicken (roughly 4 chicken breasts) cut into bite size pieces
- 4 tablespoons of butter or ghee (Indian clarified butter)
- Curry paste or spice blend (no sugar, and with no additives such as yeast extract, etc)
- 1 cup of water
- ½ cup of heavy cream or full fat coconut milk
- 1 large head of cauliflower

Procedure:

1. Melt the ghee or butter in a frying pan over medium low heat.
2. Add the spice blend or curry paste and stir to combine.
3. Add the water to the butter and spice blend over the stovetop.
4. Add the chicken and allow it to simmer for 20-25 minutes.

5. Cut the cauliflower into florets and place in a food processor. Spin until the cauliflower is chopped to small rice-sized pieces.

6. Check the chicken. If it is fully cooked and the water mostly absorbed, add the cream or coconut milk. Cook for 5-10 more minutes over low heat, stirring often.

7. Serve the curry over the cauliflower and enjoy right away!

Ketogenic Lamb Roast

Ingredients:

- Shoulder of lamb
- 3 tablespoons of olive oil
- Some fresh herbs (rosemary is recommended! Sage, basil and thyme are also a great choice.)
- 3 cloves of garlic
- A pinch of salt and pepper

Procedure:

1. In a roast pan, place the lamb. Leave any bones present in the meat in.
2. Baste with olive oil. Sprinkle with a pinch of salt and pepper.
3. Put the herbs and the garlic in the pan with the lamb shoulder.
4. Roast in the oven at 300 degrees Fahrenheit for 5 hours, or until the lamb is fully roasted and falling off the bone.
5. Transfer the lamb to a separate container.
6. Use the juices from the pan as a sauce by serving them with the lamb.
7. Serve with a salad, and steamed broccoli or asparagus.

You can also make this next recipe with any type of fish you prefer! Add spices for an extra kick!

Ketogenic Shrimp Stew

Ingredients:

- 1 pound of shrimp
- ¼ cup of olive oil
- 1 diced yellow onion
- 2 cloves of chopped garlic
- ½ cup of chopped red pepper
- 1 chopped tomato
- 1 cup coconut milk
- 1 tablespoon of lime juice
- A pinch of salt and pepper

Procedure:

1. In a saucepan, sauté the shrimp, olive oil, onion, garlic and peppers. Cook until the shrimp is no longer translucent.
2. Add the coconut milk, being careful not to bring to a boil. (Keep the ingredients simmering, but never boiling).
3. Add the salt and pepper and stir.

4. Serve with some slices of avocado on the side, and ketogenic bread slices with butter.

The next recipe is meat-free. The ketogenic is not really a good idea for vegetarians, but if you prefer to forego meat (or like to have some meat-free days, the next dish is a good one!)

Ketogenic Cheese Sticks and Veggies Vegetarian Dinner

Ingredients:

- An entire bunch of asparagus (green)
- 1 yellow onion
- 2 cloves of garlic
- 1 green bell pepper
- 1 red bell pepper
- 1 head of broccoli
- Butter for sautéing
- An entire roll of chevre cheese
- Shredded mozzarella cheese
- 1 cup of heavy cream
- A pinch of salt and pepper

Procedure:

1. Chop all of the vegetables to bite-sized pieces. Chop the garlic and onion very small.
2. Sauté all of the veggies in a frying pan with the butter.

3. When the onions are soft and translucent, add the cream and stir. Then add the two types of cheese.

4. When the cheese is melted together with the vegetables, the dish is ready!

5. Serve with a little salad or a side of bacon if you're not a vegetarian.

This next recipe is quick, easy, and full of fat and absolutely for bacon lovers!!

Bacon Sausage Wraps

Ingredients:

- 12 slices of bacon
- 4 sausages (your choice: chorizo, kielbasa, bratwurst, etc)
- Butter for frying

Procedure:

1. In a saucepan, melt the butter.
2. Wrap the sausages with the uncooked bacon so the sausages are covered in the bacon.
3. Fry the wrapped sausages until the bacon is nice and crispy.
4. Serve with sour cream and a small green salad.

Brussels sprouts are better than you ever thought! With lots of butter, garlic and onion they taste DIVINE! This next recipe is amazing and easy. Give it a chance!

Brussels Sprouts and Bacon Dinner

Ingredients:

- 3 cups of Brussels sprouts
- 6 slices of bacon
- 1 yellow onion
- 2 cloves of garlic
- Butter for frying
- A pinch of pepper

Procedure:

1. Melt the butter in a frying pan. Chop the onion and garlic. Add them to the butter.
2. Add the bacon and fry.
3. Add the Brussels sprouts and fry.
4. When the entire mixture is ready, sprinkle with pepper to taste.

Serve with sour cream and a few slices of avocado.

The typical way to eat salmon in Norway is with a cucumber salad (in vinegar) and potatoes. Since potatoes are not allowed in the ketogenic diet, we've substituted buttered cauliflower that tastes as just as good and rich! Sour cream is a traditional part of this meal, and there's no need to skimp on this high-fat diet!

Ketogenic "Norwegian" Dinner

Ingredients:

- Butter for frying
- 3 good-sized salmon filets
- 1 cucumber
- 1 head of cauliflower
- 2 Tablespoons of butter
- 2 cups of sour cream

Procedure:

1. Melt the butter in a frying pan. Add the salmon and cook over low heat.
2. Meanwhile, cut the cauliflower into florets and boil until tender. Remove from heat and add the butter.

3. Cut the cucumber into thin slices. Place in a bowl with water and add 2 tablespoons of vinegar. Sprinkle with salt and pepper.

4. Remove the salmon from the heat when it is cooked through.

5. Serve with sour cream.

6. Velbekomme! (Norwegian term for Bon Appétit!)

This recipe is great for those who love chili on cold winter days, or served cool on summer days along with a salad.

Ketogenic Chili Recipe

Ingredients:

- 1 pound of ground beef
- Butter for frying
- 2 cups of tomato paste
- ½ cup of water
- 3 cloves of garlic
- 1 onion
- Onion and garlic powder
- A pinch of pepper, cayenne pepper to taste
- 1 chopped tomato
- 1 chopped green bell pepper

Procedure:

1. Brown the ground beef with the butter in a large saucepan.
2. Add the chopped garlic, onion, tomato and pepper along with the tomato paste and the water and the spices.
3. Simmer for 25 minutes over low heat.

4. Serve with sour cream and ketogenic friendly bread (see the recipe included in this book)

Indulging Dessert Recipes

This dessert recipe is easy and fast and a delicious treat!

Ketogenic Berries and Cream Recipe

Ingredients:

- 2 cups of whipping cream
- ½ cup raspberries, blackberries or blueberries (don't exceed this amount!)
- A few drops of stevia

Procedure:

1. Put the cream in a bowl with the drops of stevia. Whip the cream.
2. Stir in the berries.
3. Serve with a sprinkle of cinnamon or vanilla powder (or vanilla scraped from a vanilla pod).

Here's an amazing cheesecake recipe! Perfect for cheesecake lovers, even those who are not on the ketogenic diet! This is 100% ketogenic and delicious.

Ketogenic Cheesecake Recipe

Ingredients:

- 16 ounces of cream cheese (two packages)
- 2 eggs
- 10 drops of stevia
- For the crust:
- 2 cups of almond flour
- 1 stick of butter, melted

Procedure:

1. Blend the almond flour with the butter. Then in a cake pan, pack the mixture down. Press evenly to the bottom of the pan.
2. Blend the eggs with the cream cheese and the stevia.
3. Bake in the oven at 350 degrees Fahrenheit for 25 minutes.
4. Chill in the freezer for two hours or overnight.
5. Serve with a handful of sliced strawberries.

Chocolate Almond Treats

Ingredients:

- 2 ounces of coconut oil
- 1 ounce of cream cheese
- 1 tablespoon of cocoa
- 10 drops of stevia
- 2 ounces of almond butter
- 1 cup of shredded coconut (optional)

Procedure:

1. Mix the coconut oil and cream cheese together with the cocoa and the stevia until smooth and well combined.
2. With a spoon, place a dollop on baking parchment (on top of a cutting board). Flatten with your hand.
3. Spoon some almond butter on top. Put a bit more coconut oil and cream cheese chocolate combination on top. Roll together with your hands. Repeat the process until you've used up all of the ingredients.
4. Optional: roll the balls in shredded coconut.

This next recipe is just as good as any classic peanut butter cookie recipe, only it's better: it's ketogenic!! Fun to make and fun to eat!

Ketogenic Peanut Butter Cookies

Ingredients:

- 2 cups of peanut butter
- 2 eggs
- ½ cup of heavy cream
- 2 tablespoons of butter
- 10 drops of stevia
- A pinch of cinnamon

Procedure:

1. Preheat the oven to 350 degrees.
2. In a bowl, combine all of the ingredients and mix with a hand mixer.
3. Put a dollop on a cookie sheet. Flatten to cookie form and repeat until all of the batter is used up.
4. Bake for 25 minutes.
5. Serve with a bit of whipped cream on top, or as is.

For those on the ketogenic diet who are craving brownies, this next recipe is just for you!

Ketogenic Chocolate Brownies

Ingredients:

- 1 cup of cream cheese
- 3 eggs
- 3 tablespoons of coconut oil
- 3 tablespoons of cocoa powder (unsweetened, of course)
- ½ cup of almond flour
- ¼ teaspoon baking soda
- ½ cup of heavy cream
- 1 teaspoon vanilla
- 1 pinch of salt

Procedure:

1. Preheat oven to 350 degrees Fahrenheit.
2. Mix the cream cheese, eggs and coconut oil, cream, and vanilla in a bowl.
3. Mix the almond flour, baking soda and cocoa powder in a separate bowl.
4. Combine the two bowls: the cream mixture with the flour mixture.

5. Grease a cake pan.

6. Add the batter to the pan and place in the oven.

7. Bake in the oven for about 35 minutes.

8. When a fork test is successful (put a fork into the brownies and when it comes out clean, it's ready).

9. Remove from the oven and cool for at least five minutes.

10. Serve with whipped cream.

This next cookie recipe is perfect for days when you want to give your oven a rest but still crave a delectable dessert!

No-Bake Ketogenic Almond Cream Cookies

Ingredients:

- 3 cups of almond flour
- 1 cup of coconut oil
- 1 tablespoon of butter
- 1 teaspoon of cinnamon
- 1 teaspoon nutmeg
- 2 cups whipping cream

Procedure:

1. In a bowl, combine the almond flour with coconut oil, butter and the cinnamon and nutmeg.
2. In another bowl, whip the whipping cream.
3. On a cookie sheet, flatten a dollop of the almond mix.
4. Add a spoonful of the cream.
5. Repeat the process until all of the ingredients have been used.

If you love berries, this next recipe is perfect for you!

Berries and Cream Ketogenic Dessert Bowl

Ingredients:

- 2 cups of fresh whipping cream
- 1 cup of raspberries
- 6 drops of stevia

Procedure:

1. Whip the cream.
2. Blend the raspberries with the stevia.
3. Combine the ingredients and serve.

Here's another recipe that's simple: pure berry bliss.

Frozen Blueberries and Cream Ketogenic Dessert

Ingredients:

- 2 cups of whipped cream
- 1 cup of frozen wild blueberries
- 6 drops of stevia

Procedure:

1. Whip the whipping cream.
2. Blend the frozen wild blueberries with the stevia. Take care to not blend for too long. You want the blueberries to remain slightly frozen and nice and cold.
3. Mix with the whipped cream.
4. Add a few leaves of fresh peppermint for a summertime treat that is refreshing and absolutely amazing!

This next dessert is another simple dish that is as delicious as it is easy. Topped with almonds, it's ketogenic and excellent.

Strawberry and Almond Ketogenic "Ice Cream"

Ingredients:

- 1 cup of frozen strawberries
- 1 cup of heavy cream
- ½ cup of chopped almonds

Procedure:

1. Blend the frozen strawberries just slightly.
2. Pour the heavy cream slowly onto the strawberries so that a layer of frozen cream forms.
3. Top with the almonds.
4. Enjoy with a dollop of whipping cream on top.
5. A good garnish idea is to add a couple of sprigs of peppermint or even basil!

Yummy Snack Recipes

This recipe is for yummy bacon snacks! The wrap the bacon forms is very easy to make.

Avocado Bacon Snacks

Ingredients:

- 12 strips of bacon
- 2 avocados

Procedure:

1. Create little baskets with the bacon by weaving the bacon together (overlapping pieces of bacon laid out together).
2. Turn the pieces up in order to form a cup (similar to the concept with the bacon tacos. Google bacon weave if you are uncertain as to how to do this)
3. Bake in the oven.
4. When the bacon is ready, fill with avocado slices and eat on the go.

The next recipe is for a fast and good warm snack!

Gruyere Onion Snacks

Ingredients:

- Butter for frying
- 2 large onions cut into rings
- 1 cup of gruyere cheese

Procedure:

1. Melt the butter in a frying pan.
2. Add the onion rings and sauté until translucent.
3. Add the gruyere cheese.
4. Warm the mass until the cheese is partially melted.
5. Sprinkle with a bit of pepper and some herbs such as basil or thyme, oregano or dill, onion powder, garlic powder, etc.

The next recipe is truly fast and easy and is also super for lunch on the go, or for breakfast with an herbal tea.

Ham and Cheese Rolls with Cucumber bits

Ingredients:

- 4 pieces of ham cold cuts
- 4 pieces of thinly sliced cheese of your choice
- Cucumber cut into bits, drizzled with olive oil
- 1 tablespoon of cream cheese

Procedure:

1. Combine the cream cheese and the cucumber with the olive oil in a bowl.
2. Put together a slice of ham with a slice of cheese and top with the cucumber and cream cheese mixture.
3. Roll up the slices and repeat the process until all of the ingredients have been integrated.

This next recipe is for homemade roasted almonds! It only requires a few ingredients, is simple and satisfying to take with you on the go to munch on between meals.

Ketogenic Roasted Salted Almonds

Ingredients:

- 2 pounds of almonds
- 2 tablespoons of Himalaya salt
- 1 tablespoon of garlic powder
- 2 tablespoons of olive oil

Procedure:

1. Place the almonds and salt in a bowl with just enough water to cover.
2. Let the almonds soak for about 7 hours or overnight.
3. Drain the water and put in a cookie sheet with baking parchment.
4. Drizzle with a bit of olive oil.
5. Sprinkle with a pinch more of salt and the garlic powder.
6. Bake in the oven at 150 degrees Fahrenheit for4 hours or until the almonds are sufficiently dry. (Taste test to ensure they are prepared to your taste)

This next recipe is another easy snack that tastes so hearty and satisfying that even makes for a great light meal.

Zucchini Snacks

Ingredients:

- 2 zucchini
- Butter for frying
- Garlic powder (1 teaspoon)
- Onion powder (1 teaspoon)
- A pinch of dill
- 2 tablespoons of goat cheese

Procedure:

1. Slice the zucchini into thin slices.
2. Melt the butter in a frying pan over the stove.
3. Add the garlic and onion powder and dill.
4. Add the goat cheese to the mixture. Sautee a moment more and serve in a bowl. Serves 2 people, or 1 with leftovers. Also makes a great light lunch. Real bacon bits are a tasty addition to this simple and satisfying dish.

Here's a delicious snack recipe that is quite versatile.

Sautéed Spinach and Cream Cheese Dip
(Served with ketogenic bread rolls or bread slices)

Ingredients:

- 2 cups of spinach
- 2 tablespoons of butter
- 2 cloves of garlic
- 1 onion
- 2 cups of cream cheese
- A pinch of salt and pepper

Procedure:

1. In a frying pan, fry the onions and garlic with the butter.
2. As the onions and garlic are tender, add the spinach.
3. Stir to combine well, and add the cream cheese.
4. When well-combined, remove from heat and serve. A perfect topping to ketogenic rolls or bread! Or as a sauce or side to steak and other meat dishes.

Quenching Smoothie Recipes

Here we have a few delicious, simple and fulfilling smoothie recipes for smoothie fans who have committed to the ketogenic diet.

Buttermilk Cocoa Ketogenic Smoothie

Ingredients:

- 3 cups of buttermilk
- 1 tablespoon of cocoa
- A pinch of cinnamon
- 6 drops of stevia
- A few ice cubes

Procedure:

1. In a blender, combine all of the ingredients.
2. Top with whipped cream for an extra special treat!

Blueberry Buttermilk Ketogenic Smoothie

Ingredients:

- 3 cups of buttermilk
- ¼ cup of wild blueberries
- 6 drops of stevia
- A few ice cubes

Procedure:

1. In your blender, combine all of the ingredients until smooth.
2. Serve with whipped cream for a treat, or drink as is.

Peanut Butter Chocolate Cream Dream Ketogenic Smoothie

Ingredients:

- 2 cups of buttermilk
- 1 cup of heavy cream
- 1 tablespoon of peanut butter
- 1 tablespoon of cocoa
- A few ice cubes
- 6 drops of stevia

Procedure:

1. In a blender, combine all of the ingredients. Blend until smooth.
2. Serve cold, with whipped cream or as is.

Coconut Cream Berry Bliss Ketogenic Smoothie

Ingredients:

- 2 cups coconut milk (unsweetened, natural)
- 1 cup of heavy cream
- 1 teaspoon of vanilla
- ¼ a cup of blackberries
- 6 drops of stevia

Procedure:

1. In a blender, blend all of the ingredients until smooth.
2. Serve cold with whipped cream.

Forest Berry Ketogenic Smoothie

Ingredients:

- 2 cups of coconut milk
- 1 cup of heavy cream
- 2 cup of blackberries, blueberries and raspberries
- A few ice cubes
- 6 drops of stevia

Procedure:

1. Combine the ingredients in a blender. Blend until smooth.
2. Serve simply as is or with a topping of whipped cream.

Conclusion

The Ketogenic diet may seem daunting, but with a book of delicious recipes it is really quite easy! Just follow the recipes to stay or get to the optimal state of ketosis, while enjoying yummy meals with friends or family or alone. Burn fat while eating lots of fat! It's really fun when you think about it.

The ketogenic diet helps to efficiently and quickly lose weight, achieve clear skin, prevent cancer, and heal MS, Parkinson's and more. It is possible for anyone to go on this diet and get great results. The health benefits are numerous. Keeping them firmly in mind will help you stay on track, inspired and motivated to keep going.

The typical ketogenic meal is high in fat, which means it is satisfying and filling. This isn't a diet where you need to go hungry! With this diet book as your guide, you can lose the weight you've always wanted to get rid of but couldn't. The recipes spanning everything from healthy dinners including fresh salads, to rich desserts and creamy smoothies, following the recipes guarantees success in weight loss.

In our society, we are taught that fat is the enemy. We learn through experience, that this isn't true and that a huge helping of cream, bacon or coconut oil does us good, and tastes great at that! Our ancestors ate a lot of fat until society switched over to a more carb-based, grain-filled diet which has only proven to be unhealthy and to cause and feed many conditions. Going back to what our ancestors ate allows the body to reset, to use fat as fuel and get away from the unhealthy legacy that is sugar.

We wish you the best of luck with your diet endeavors! The ketogenic diet is the most efficient one you can find, for burning fat and fixing your health.

Sincerely,

Sara Elliott Price

Made in the USA
San Bernardino, CA
10 February 2016